How to Have Fun on Halloween

By Cindy Wright

ISBN: 13:978-1724455246

Contents

What is Halloween?

Everyone has heard of Halloween, and over the years, children have been frightful when seeing all those scary costumes. For us grown-ups now, there may be memories of Trick or Treating and fun times from parties with family and friends. After all our celebrations, it is not always apparent to most about the origin of Halloween and how its true nature began. So, the question is, "What is Halloween really?"

To begin answering this question, you could start tracing the ancient roots of the Celtic pagan feast of Samhain, including the Christian holiday of All Saints' Day. Mostly, it is considered as a secular celebration. Over the years, many have had strong positive and negative feelings towards the religious association. Our modern Halloween celebrations here in the UK, came across the water from the United States, but their origins began when Irish immigrants took the tradition with them to North America during the Great Irish Famine of the 1840s.

The Samhain is a Gaelic festival that comes from an old Irish word meaning Summer's End. This celebrates the end of the lighter half (spring and summer) of the year, before returning to the darker half (autumn and winter). So back in history, people even named this the "Celtic New Year". Samhain, also, encouraged people to start stocking their houses with food, as well as slaughtering their livestock, and their bones thrown on to bonfires. During the day and night, house fires were extinguished, so that their rooms were lit only by the bonfires.

The word Halloween is derived from the phrase "All Hallow Even, but over the years Even originally Evening, has now been shorted to E'en. This was originally derived from the Old English Phrase "Eallra Halgen Afen". This term is now known as "All Saints' Day. Halloween coincides with this day on the 1st of November, which is why Halloween is celebrated on the 31st October being its Eve. The Catholic Church in the 800s AD, begin the day at sunset, according to the Florentine calendar.

In modern times, Halloween is seen as the Festival of the Dead. The Ancient Gael believed that the Samhain was the dividing line between our world and the other worlds. The belief was that spirits came through and roamed freely among our world, which could be both harmless and harmful, which is in some ways related to All Saints' and All Souls' Day. The idea of wearing scary masks and costumes was to ward off these evil spirits.

Our Halloween of today has created a new tradition that involves a lot more fun. This fun comes in the form of trick or treating, ghost tours, bonfires, costume parties, pranks, watching horror movies and telling ghost stories. Some of these have scared us, as well our children of today, but now more ideas of fun are opening up each year making it enjoyable for them once again. The traditional universal colours of Halloween are now known to be orange and black, such as the symbol of Jack o' Lantern.

Acting scared on Halloween has now become customary as part of its fun. People are getting more and more creative each year making it unique to their own celebrations. You can even make the food at parties blend in with the theme. Celebrating Halloween can be effective and practical fun without it costing a fortune. Each year

is getting more and more interesting, and not forgetting
the fun.

What Do You Think About Halloween?

Halloween is the time of year when spooky stories are told, and our favourite movies watched. It is becoming one of the most celebrated occasions, even here in the UK. As October approaches, people worldwide begin to think about how they will be celebrating, and everyone has their own unique style. Religion has no association with the tradition, and Halloween has no identity with race.

Now Halloween means fun for the children. They can go around their local areas dressed in spooky costumes with friends trick or treating. Tricks are probably furthest from their minds, as most people will be handing out sweets and chocolate, and seeing who gets the most at the end of the evening. People's homes and gardens are decorated too, even if it's just a pumpkin on the doorstep to share in the fun, whether they have children themselves or not.

Teenagers will probably have no excuses when it comes to helping family and friends organise a Halloween party. To them it's a wonderful time to socialise with their friends, eat lots of party food and perhaps a little dancing. It can be tiring for the grown-ups, who have endless meetings with others to organise their festivities. In the end, their time and money is all worth it as they can eventually relax and join in the fun.

If you are not arranging any kind of festivity, it's still a great time to watch others having fun. Even if it's just watching all the children roaming around in their costumes, and collecting their treats or maybe observing how other gardens and houses have been decorated to give you more ideas for the next get-to-gether.

Halloween for Children and Teenagers

 Not everyone can go out roaming the streets visiting houses, especially the smaller children and toddlers. It can be stressful when parents are trying to watch them, as well as keep an eye on their older children. Children of all ages still need a parent or grown-up to accompany them to make sure they are safe, and in no kind of danger. If you cannot find a suitable person to look after your younger children, or go with the ones who are older, you may need to think of alternative ways on how you celebrate your Halloween. There are still lots of ways you can celebrate and have fun in the safety of your own home.

Here are some ideas you may like to try:

1.   *Halloween Crafting*

This is great for small children and toddlers. They will love colouring and making different shapes. You could help them make their own Halloween mask, so that they can wear it while eating dinner or when visiting relatives the next day. Cut all the pieces and shapes out in preparation for the day, so all they have to do is paste and organise their craft, and don't forget to include lots of different colours. If you want, you can ask them what kind of mask they would like to make a few days before, so that you can have everything ready for the task.

An idea for a mask is to use a paper plate, and to cut eyes and mouths in it to look like a Jack o' Lantern. Use staples to secure rubber bands or strings to keep the mask on. If your child doesn't like wearing masks, you could make pumpkin decorations out of them using glitter, yarn, fabric and glue.

2.   *Cake Baking*

All children enjoy helping Mum bake. They can help you bake a Halloween themed cake you can eat after dinner. Get them to help decorate it, and make it the table's centrepiece. Cupcakes and buns are also a great idea. There are many sugar decorations you can buy these days that can be used, such as bats, spiders and black cats. You can even try cookies, if you wish.

Use cookie cutters, food colouring, liquorice, icing, patterns and macaroni to make ghoulish faces. Use green jelly or a milk pudding with food colouring to make slime.

Whatever it is you decide to bake get the children involved, so they can feel a part of the celebration.

3. *Scaring People from Your House*

 You don't have to go out of your house to enjoy trick or treating. Remember, your doorbell will ring a few times as well when your neighbours know you are home. Get your children dressed in a scary costume, and when visitors arrive at your house get the children helping you to greet, scare and pass out the treats. They will enjoy it just as much as the ones walking around. The dressing up part alone is great fun for them.

When a child yourself, you must have had some fond Halloween memories, as do I. Although trick or treating wasn't as common back then, but we had great family and friend parties with lots of food and barbecues. If it wasn't for these, Halloween to us was just a normal day. We made our own fun back then, and you still can today. If you went knocking on people's front doors then, someone would have come out yelling and scaring you off. Now people expect it, and if you don't want to join in the fun, you don't have to open the door. Now there is excitement all around as the build up to Halloween gets closer.

Costumes are fun, some have their own originality or you could go for the more traditional, such as ghosts, witches, monsters, super heroes, vampires and magicians. Whatever you choose, you can still make it unique when playing around with make-up.

Although Halloween is mostly for our children to have fun, but what about our teenagers! If they are not going out with younger siblings, they will have some other kind of fun up their sleeves to celebrate. Some will organise some sort of dance event or a concert. They may begin to impress the opposite sex when choosing their costumes or they may just want to hang out with their friends. Whatever their choice respect them, and let them have fun.

Over the years, the Halloween tradition has become one of the most important events every year. Children and teenagers may become the most excited, but secretly grown-ups can look forward to the tradition too.

Preparations Simple and on a Budget

 If you are reading this book, Halloween must be around the corner and you are starting to think about preparing the house, garden, food, treats and the all-important costumes. Many people are struggling financially these days, but that doesn't mean you can't enjoy a little Halloween fun. We don't want our children to miss out when all their friends are celebrating.

Have a look at these fun and stress free ideas:

1.   *Use Last Year's Ideas*

Reusing does not have to mean the same. Try to come up with different ways of decorating, like putting them in a different area of the house or just use them differently. Old outfits that are not suitable for wearing anywhere else can be changed into a scarecrow or use it as a decoration for the wall. Using the same bag or basket, you used last year to carry your treats will not be the end of the world if used again and again. Make this year less stressful on you, and your budget. If you used a vampire costume last year, and it no longer fits then try using the cape as a table runner instead. You could always use a witch's hat as a treat basket as well.

2.   *Think Halloween All Year Round*

Try not to wait until the last minute before preparing your celebrations. Look out for clothes you are throwing out that no longer fit your child. Think if you can make them into something else. Take advantage of sales and discounted items throughout the year. Maybe start straight after Halloween, as most of the decorations sold in shops will be on sale to get rid of their stock. Look for artificial spider webs and glow in the dark skeletons. Hang these all over the house to create a spooky atmosphere. As long as you have a safe space to store all your items, this should be a great time and cost saving activity.

3.   *Involving Family*

It is so much more fun when preparing these events with family. You can all agree to do one task each, so the jobs are smaller. At the same time, the children get to hang out with you and enjoy being a part of it. It will also be a learning experience for them, knowing what is actually involved in organising a party.

4.   *Make your own*

If your child is only wearing their costume for a few hours, and won't be going on to a party, then buying something expensive will not work. To get ideas look at some YouTube videos, magazines and craft books. There should be some ideas around to help you make your treat bags and place cards for your party table. There are usually lots of things around the home you can use to make something less expensive.

Inexpensive Halloween Decorations

 Without decorations, celebrating Halloween would be boring, just like trying to celebrate Christmas without putting up our tree. It just wouldn't be the same. In the past, people believed that the putting up of decorations was very important, as they would help drive away those evil spirits. Now they are just part of tradition, and nothing otherworldly involved.

Halloween Candlelight

Using candles is probably one of the cheapest decorations around. Purchase a big bag of tea lights, and use them in a decorative container or make your own. Light them up all over the house, and don't forget to light up your pumpkins. You could use drinking glasses and small vases as holders too, as this will create an eerie atmosphere.

Place a few broken twigs next to the candles (remembering safety first) as these will add to that atmosphere creating shadows.

Home Made Creatures

Remember me talking about that scarecrow a few chapters back. Get all your old clothes and newspaper strips and tie them together with a belt, threads or safety pins. Use a balloon tied up with string for its head or a stuffed pillowcase. Then stick shapes on its face, and add a hat. There you go you've made yourself a Halloween monster.

Other Ideas

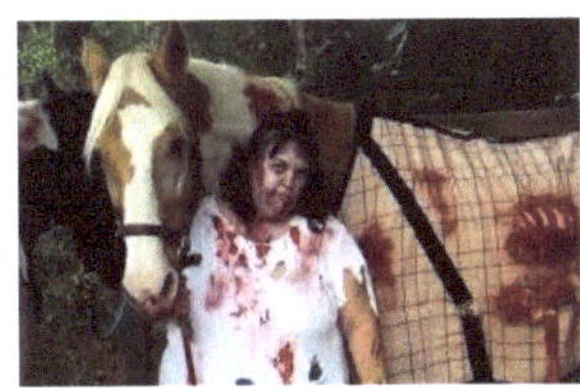 If you can get some marshmallows, use them to make great ghost figure decorations. If you remember The Marshmallow man in "Ghostbusters", you will know what I mean.

Another way to give the illusion of a ghost is by using tissues that you could paint faces on.

Find some old gauze, and use it to make a Mummy. Make some Mummy treats too; by wrapping dough sheets round hotdog pieces the children will love them. To make them spookier draw eyes and mouths on them with tomato sauce.

If you haven't been able to find any artificial spider's webs make some of your own. Try weaving some black cotton together to give the same effect.

Maybe you want to make a graveyard as your theme. Use cardboard boxes, like empty cereal packets, cover them in paper and get your children to decorate them.

Perhaps you could use a crystal ball as a centrepiece for any party table. Pretend to be a fortune teller, and tell some horror stories. Use creepy shadows or glowing eyes at windows to make it look like someone is looking in. Use lighting such as candles to add to the effect. Don't forget to record some scary sounds.

Making your Child's Costume without Spending a Fortune

A few inexpensive ideas to help dress up your child this Halloween. If you are on a budget, there are still ways you can be very creative. Check out the following examples.

1. *Ghost* - I'm sure most of you are aware of how to make the perfect ghost costume for your child. The white sheet technique. Again, this is so inexpensive, because most of us have old white sheets around the house. Cut out some holes for their eyes, and use marker pens to drawn on blood,

spider webs, chains and anything you can think of to make it spooky.

2.   *Hobo* – Does your husband have any old clothes they only use for dirty jobs, such as gardening or tinkering with their cars? Find an outdated hat that matches them to add to the effect. Use face paint to give your child a beard to add the effect of them being older.

3.   *Nerd* – These are always in films and TV programmes, so chances are your child is familiar with the term. You need some old fashioned clothes that are not designer made. They could wear trousers that look too tight, and shirts buttoned to the top. Your child's hairstyle is definitely the key to this look. Use gel to smooth it, and make it flat to the head. Next, you can add some old glasses to complete the look. On the day of Halloween, they

can carry around smart looking books to add to the
nerd effect.

4.   *Angel* – We don't always have to dress up as an
Angel at Christmas time. They are great Halloween
costumes too. The same idea as for a ghost using a
sheet will work great. Instead of spooky makeup,
glue glitter to the sheet. Then create some wings
and a halo, and there you have an angel.

A Different Way of Celebrating

 In the Philippines, they celebrate Halloween in a unique way. Being a rare Christian Asian nation, they do it with a twist. They celebrate for over two days on the 1st and 2nd November. They call it All Saints' Day and All Souls' Day like many Catholic nations of the world.

During Halloween, the Filipinos visit the graveyards of their deceased relatives instead of going trick or treating. The days are spent in prayer. The graves of their loved ones are decorated, as well as their extravagant mausoleums where they are housed.

They light candles around the graves while they pray as a religious symbolism. These lights will help prayers reach their relatives. They will remain lit even during daytime hours. They make it a real family affair with food and recreational items. They turn it into a fantastic celebration with dancing, eating and socialising.

Teenagers have their own way of celebrating here too. They go door to door like trick or treating serenading the homeowners (a bit like carol singing at Christmas). Instead of getting sweets and chocolate they would get money that they would give to a church or a charity. Modern celebrations are now starting to catch up with the Filipinos and they are adopting these fun ways.

If you want to celebrate Halloween and make it a spooky event, maybe you could spend time in a graveyard if the church allows it.

Halloween Party Games

1. A Brain Game – You should be able to find a rubber  brain in a joke or toyshop. Alternatively, make one yourself with jelly, and fill it with gummy sweets, such as worms and other little trinkets and gifts. Get your child to dig in and pick them out.

2. Spaghetti Game – Make sure your children are wearing an apron or some other garment to protect their clothes before you start playing. Cook a large bowl of spaghetti, and fill it with things such as plastic bugs, gummy worms and other things you can find. Let the children put their hands in to see if they can identify what they touch and feel. Once everything is cleaned up then get them to list what they can remember, and then give out a prize for the most remembered.

3.   Another game is to paint a cardboard box in black, inside and out. Cut a small hole in the top that's just big enough for a child's hand, and fill it with a selection of goodies. To make it more interesting place items in the box that can feel like body parts or brain matter. Then the children can put their hands in the box to identify the items. The reward for remembering the most items can be the box or a prize.

4.   If your children, have a vivid imagination maybe they would like to put it down on paper. Let them write a scary, silly story. Then on the day of the party get them to read a different story out to family and friends. Then see if they tell each other who wrote which story.

5.   Children love word games relating to a certain time of the year or celebration. You could use the word

Halloween or a longer one that they can use to find as many other words in it as possible. Put a time limit on the game, and the child with the most words in that time gets a prize.

Keeping Safe during Halloween

Halloween is a fun annual event, but it can soon turn into a nightmare if people are not careful. There will be a lot of children running around in the dark, and they can easily become lost or worse kidnapped.

There are some parents who don't see the danger during events like this. They believe that if their children are still in the neighbourhood no harm will become them.

Some tips to help their safety:

1.   Buddy System - There should be at least one adult  for every child, so they will have eyes on them at all times. If the children, are 8 years old or above you could have one adult to two children.

2.   If you know of a responsible teenager, they could be a great companion for your child. If the teenager

tends to be a little wild, it would be better if they were not caring for your child. Make sure they are mature enough to stay with your child, and not wander off to do their own things. If you use a baby sitter, make sure their credentials are up to the mark.

3. Start out early with your children, even if it's still light outside, so that there are not many people about. This way your children will be easier to manage. If they are not happy about this, tell them there will be more sweets for the early birds, and then when they come home they can help out giving treats to their own visitors that come to the door.

4. We all know that the darker scarier costume is more appealing, but have them dress up in

something lighter and brighter, so that they are easier to be seen and stand out in the crowd.

If you adopt some of my ideas that are present in this book or not, I hope, you have a fun packed Halloween this year.